G. H. (George Herbert) Powell

Occasional Rhymes & Reflections

Upon Subjects Social, Literary and Political

G. H. (George Herbert) Powell

Occasional Rhymes & Reflections
Upon Subjects Social, Literary and Political

ISBN/EAN: 9783337078751

Printed in Europe, USA, Canada, Australia, Japan

Cover: Foto ©Thomas Meinert / pixelio.de

More available books at **www.hansebooks.com**

OCCASIONAL
RHYMES & REFLECTIONS

UPON SUBJECTS

SOCIAL, LITERARY, AND POLITICAL.

BY

G. H. POWELL,

OF THE INNER TEMPLE.

REVISED AND CORRECTED, WITH NOTES.

LONDON:
LAWRENCE & BULLEN,
16, HENRIETTA STREET, COVENT GARDEN, W.C.
MDCCCXCII.

LONDON:
HENDERSON & SPALDING (LIMITED), GENERAL PRINTERS,
3 & 5, MARYLEBONE LANE, OXFORD STREET, W.

TO THE READER.

THE following verses are, for the most part, selected from a larger number contributed to various journals (the *St. James's Gazette* in particular) during the past three or four years. A good many, however, are here printed for the first time. Those dealing with political subjects represent (as it appears to the author) only such Reflections upon political incidents, views, and characters of the day as must commonly have suggested themselves to the average Englishman of moderately Liberal principles.

Of the " Rhymes " as a whole, it may be added that, though mainly of a would-be amusing nature, the serious has not been excluded, nor such variety both of manner and matter as, it is hoped, may succeed in satisfying some section of the indulgent public.

G. H. P.

2, THANET PLACE,
   TEMPLE BAR,
     May 4, 1892.

TABLE OF CONTENTS.

	PAGE
Our River	1
To J. Russell Lowell	5
The "Friend of Humanity"	8
A Counsel of Perfection	12
A Dream of the Armed Continent	15
To Walt Whitman	17
A Song of Storms	19
A Spring Madrigal	22
The Goal of —*Jacobinism!*	24
An Incident of the Agrarian Campaign	27
The Passionate Female Suffragist to his Love	30
The Legislative "Organ"	32
A Conundrum	34
Lines Attributed to W. E. A. S.	36
Contentment—An Ode	39
A Nursery Rhyme	41
A Wail from "New Tipperary"	42

TABLE OF CONTENTS.

	PAGE
A Dramatic Idyll	44
My Love's Hat	50
Lines to a Young Law Student	53
A Ballad of the Thames	56
The Laureate at Bay	61
After Bret Harte	65
The "Leading Magazine"	67
The Lay of the Advertiser	70
A Ballade of Ballade-mongers	72
The Modern Armourer's Carol	75
In the Zoo.—By a "Minor" Poet	77
To an Eminent *Littérateur*	80
A Song of Self-defence	83
Horatian Ode	86
At a Post Office.—By G. M.	89
To a Thoughtful Editor	92
Ode to the Electric Light	94
Conversational Ditties :—	
1. The Flat Joke	96
2. The Man who Knows	96

RHYMES AND REFLECTIONS.

OCCASIONAL RHYMES AND REFLECTIONS.

OUR RIVER.

O RIVER, our river!
    Full thirty years ago
All through the golden summers
    I watched your peaceful flow.
How many a gleam across your face,
    How many a cloud, would pass,
Till the white mists rolled up to hide
    Its darkling magic glass.

How quiet, how eerie,
    The oily waters grey,
Where once an hour the sombre pike
    Burst upward on his prey;

Or shoals of darting minnows
   Left laggards in the lurch,
When bristling through the shallows
   Flamed in the splendid perch.

O'er the broad waters rarely
   Came sound of human speech,
What time the sleepy barges
   Drooped down the basking reach.
Perchance a Don from Oxford
   In flannels and white tie,
Or pair of Ancient Mariners
   Would swing severely by.

The tripper, the tripper,
   Theirs is our river now,
Furrowed from morn to even
   By many a vagrant prow.

3

Launch after launch unceasing
   Wash fry and banks away,
And thrice a thousand Cockneys
   Splash through the Sabbath day.

But yet in mild October
   And after heavy showers,
When cautious cheap excursionists
   Fear Pluvius's powers ;
When many a noisy oarsman
   Hard at his desk is set,
The river, dear river,
   It is our river yet.

Once more they glide before me,
   The oily waters grey,
Scarce ruffled save when perch or pike
   Strike sudden on the prey.

4

The quiet brings a glamour,
    Wild nature's ancient grace,
And the white mist rolls up to hide
Our river's silent face.

TO J. RUSSELL LOWELL.*

(August, 1891.)

FAREWELL, good friend, from that strange land,
    The heir of Europe's hopes and fears,
In thine we grasped thy country's hand :
    —How strange her wrinkled youth appears,
Though wrought into a manlier mould
    By that fierce furnace of the war,
Yet worshipping dull calves of gold,
    And trusting blindly to her star.

Outrage that plucks the beard of law,
    Fierce factions waging soulless strife,
Coarse wiles old England never saw,
    And heartless Fraud that plays with life :

---

* Whose death, it will be remembered, occurred not very long after certain disgraceful disturbances in Philadelphia.

—What wild tare-harvest rank and drear
    Yet hides the swelling seed of Fate,
Soul of the race these lands must rear,
    To make and keep their mighty State.

Farewell, true scion of the stock,
    Once fainting England's moral salt ;
Brave leader, steadfast as the rock
    'Gainst idiot anarchy's assault.
Bright scorn that never made a foe,
    True laugh that woke man's better part,
With wholesome passion's trenchant flow,
    Warm-blooded from the homely heart.

Farewell, yet not the last is gone
    Of those who trusted that the day
Of true Democracy should dawn
    With somewhat of a fuller ray :

Who, proudest of a land to be,
 Still taught the young world from the old
And hoped and strove for what his free
 New pure Republic shall unfold.

THE "FRIEND OF HUMANITY" IN THE PROVINCES.*

(1891.)

POOR rural voter! which way are you voting?
    Sombre and dark the political horizon,
Blank is the outlook, and I fancy you are
    Scarcely contented?

Downtrodden peasant! do you think the landlords,
Who in their coaches drive you to the poll-booth,
Know what hard work 'tis digging all the day in
    Cottage allotments?

---

* *Vide* the reports of the "Special Commissioner" despatched by a leading Radical organ during the dead season of last year to inquire into the state of the rural districts. This gentleman was instructed to discover that the depopulation of " our villages" was

Tell me, poor voter, how you came to *be* poor.
Was it some rich man robbed you of your birthright?
Ignorant rustic! know you the whole earth be-
    longs to the "People"?

How do your children get their education?
Under the hateful "voluntary" system?
Must they, when bid by some sectarian teacher,
    Learn the commandments?

Need you, when Parson or the Curate passes,
Doff your worn hat to proud ecclesiastics?
Do the Squire's blankets gall your manly spirit?
    What is your grievance?

owing to local tyranny and bigotry. He unfortunately discovered as well that the rustic voter wanted "allotments," which a Conservative Government were already giving him. This mistake was quickly and adroitly rectified by the substitution of "Village Parliaments," &c., &c., as the essentials of rural felicity.

The Rural Voter.

Grievance? Lor' bless you ! — why, the custed
   weather !
—Parson a' bin 'ere more na foorty year, sir :
Main poor he be ; and what he has he mostly
      Spends on the parish.

It ain't the Squire, whatever you may think, sir.
But Mister Byles, the Nonconformist grocer,
Has the bad cottage just below the green there,
      Worse nor a pigsty.

'Taint the poor landlords drives the folk to Lunnun ;
All the young chaps goes theer to seek a fortin.
Varmin' doant pay : and there's the long and short of
      Depopulation.

FRIEND OF HUMANITY (*aside*).

Slave of the soil, unworthy to be rescued
From the base bondage of the Feudal system!

(*Musing, as he returns to town, and arranges notes for the forthcoming " report."*)

—Doesn't this show the scandalous extent of
Tory corruption?

A COUNSEL OF PERFECTION.

Addressed to an Official Bungler at the Admiralty, Treasury, or elsewhere, by an Opposition Idealist.

NAY, nay, no more. Though years may roll,
    Our feelings are not changed by time.
Yours is perchance a kindly soul
    As yet unsteeped in blackest crime;
But yet you are (we've told you so)
A base, designing, dangerous foe.

Your latest fond and foolish scheme
    Of Tax, Reform, or Armament
May be—(yet all too wild the dream)
    No, no; it cannot be—well meant.
But if it were, we all agree
'Tis just as bad as it can be.

The chronic scare, the wild alarm
    With sober prudence to abjure
The while from every risk of harm
    Betimes to make the land secure—
We cherished once that grand design :
What *yours* may mean we can't divine.

We know you for a hireling crew
    Consumed by vulgar selfish greed.
How can we bear that such as you
    Should bungle where we might succeed?
We wonder that you should not see
How base your every act must be.

'Tis true—of knowledge, strength, and skill
    Some crumbs have fallen to your share ; .
Your names to puff, your purse to fill,
    'Twould seem you've neither need nor care.
It may be so,—a specious blind
That covers something worse behind.

We weep that you should be so vile,
    Your virtue such a tinsel gaud,
Your prudence fraught of fear and guile,
    Your candour mask for glaring fraud;
But fate's decree has ordered thus,
That wisdom lives, and dies, with us.

A DREAM OF THE ARMED CONTINENT.*

IT was a monster armament,
    So mighty and bright and keen :
A spear in rest, and a bow full bent,
    A murderous man-machine :
And it hung and swayed like a Damocles' blade
    O'er the anxious-peaceful scene.

And the Ruler waked in the night
    For thought of the Balance of Power.
"Though no deadly ball on my ramparts fall,
    Can I wait one fateful hour?
Can I trust to the foe the first dread blow
    When threatening storm-clouds lower?"

* "It is estimated that Germany could in a week set 750,000 men in French territory. . . . . Over twenty millions of Europeans are liable to expose their lives in the next great war. Would they do it? That is a question which must sometimes puzzle the brains of the statesmen who believe that they pull the wires of this vast and murderous apparatus."—Daily Paper, Oct. 1889.

Then he thrilled the electric line
  To the armament marshalled there—
"Ho! fall on the foe, great engine of mine,
  And scatter their pride to air"
(And add one wrong more to the perilous store
  Of vengeance and fierce despair).

But the mighty machine, unmoved,
  Made answer with passionate cries,
"Shall a man pay toll of the life of his soul
  For the conqueror's bloodstained prize?"
And the man-machine grew wise,
  And the death-bearing bow unbent;
For the nation's heart would no more be part
  Of a "monster armament."

TO WALT WHITMAN

IN HEAVEN.

WHEN first across the Atlantic's roll
    We caught your carols so fresh and strong,
What souls sprang upward to greet your soul,
    The bard whose coming we waited long!

" 'Twas a dream "—they tell us—" the years that pass
    Bring no more prophets with old-world powers:
—And what is a leaflet of prairie grass
    To the glowing garden of Europe's flowers?"

—Not ours to praise you, the earthborn Man,
    Serenely mighty, superbly sweet,
—To defend your page from the blatant ban
    Of a pigmy peering about your feet:

—Ah! never. Not if I grasped your hand
    With the love of a comrade, proud and free,
It is no strange bard from a far-off land,
    But the new world-spirit that speaks to me;

—But a quick suggestion, a glance of fire,
    A sign, a miracle, a delight;
Just shown to us here as we strive and tire,
    Then folded into the folds of night.

O soft sweet singers of golden lays,
    Ye gave us freely of all your store:
But I treasure above your brightest bays
    This pebble from " blue Ontario's shore."

A SONG OF STORMS.

(*Nov.* 9, 1890.)*

FIERCE the northern winter,
    Dark the western sky,
Hark ! across the low'ring tempest
    Peals a seaward cry.
'Gainst the hurricane's fierce onset,
    Serried breakers jar ;
Peasants, miners turn to wage
    Elemental war.

---

* The reader may remember that on this day (a Sunday) a terrific gale swept over the west coast, involving in destruction all kinds of sea-going craft, from the nobleman's yacht (dragging her anchors all night and cast away in the morning) to the collier-brig dashed helplessly on the rocks, and going down with all hands. The newspapers of the next morning were crowded with descriptions of "Terrible Loss of Life," "Heroic Rescues," and "Attempts at Rescue." The latter, on the part of persons, artisans and quarrymen, leaving their ordinary inland vocations to take part in these perilous enterprises, were sufficiently remarkable to deserve some more durable memorial.

England's soul makes answer
    To that dying call !
Poor and wealthy, gentle, simple—
    Victims each and all,
Snared to-night by storm and darkness
    In one dreadful net,
To those sleepless billows
    Pay our mighty debt.

So, when fiercely sundered
    From the lands at rest,
Sea-bred mother, clasp thy children
    Closer to thy breast.
Joys and fears of unknown heroes,
    Manhood's pride and pain,
Weld the might of ocean
    To thy soul again.

Howl, oh storm and tempest ;
    Let thy stress prolong
Nature's one supreme alliance,
    Britain, true and strong.
Round her rocky coasts re-echo,
    Shake the cloudy dome ;
On this island-anvil
    Beat our one-ness home.

A SPRING MADRIGAL.*

YOUNG May went forth, with bud and flower,
    To meet the sun at trysting due ;
" He hath not now his ancient power,
    Let others fail, yet I am true."

Ah me ! none gave a warning cry
    As she stepped forth so blithe and gay ;
A gang of villain winds came by :
    With bitter stabs they murdered May.

With bitter stabs they murdered May,
    And lapped her in a chilly sheet,
And cast her in the whirling way
    Of flooded waters, fast and fleet.

* Suggested by the singular weather tragedy concluded May 30, 1891.

Fierce Summer flashed a fiery eye
 Of angry light that lit her shroud.
And, as dead May went whirling by,
 He frowned, and wept, and groaned aloud.

The wroth Sun caught the villain crew,
 And struggling, turned a dusky red :
"Who killed my May? 'Twas you, 'twas you!"
 And, fainting, sank upon his bed.

* * * * *

Then woke aflush with glad surprise
 —'Twas but a dream of winter drear.
It is no wraith that mocks our eyes,
 But late the longed-for May is here.

Is here? Is fled. Nay, let her fly ;
 (Ring in the new) for we behold
The full year's pageant sweeping by
 With glories of the days of old.

THE GOAL OF—JACOBINISM?

[" True Liberalism "—*sed quære if the above be not a preferable reading*—" is never satisfied."—*Daily News.*]

YOU ask me why, so ill at ease,
    In this dull region I persist
    (With spirits damper than the mist),
In projects wilder than the breeze.
It is because, through good or ill,
    One principle is still my guide,
That whatsoe'er the people's will,
    It never shall be " satisfied."

Though power should make from land to land
    The name of Britain trebly great,
    I care not for Imperial State,
And oh, still less for " golden sand."

To smooth the waves of discontent
    May fill a humbler heart with pride ;
'Tis mine to give all passions vent,
    And keep them never satisfied.

Each evil to its ghastly root
    I trace with all unclouded ken ;
See women hung'ring to be men,
    And ploughboys for a village-moot.
And naught my energies shall daunt
    (Ratepaying matters not to me)
Till everything they do not want
    Is furnished to the "masses"—*free*.

Or else, on changeful prospects bent
    I'd seek some bracing Celtic shore,
    Where, torn by factions evermore,
Meets the bi-weekly Parliament ;

While rotted by a sneering blight,
    All true and tried tradition lies,
And full grown in a single night
    The legislative fungi rise.

    *   *   *   *   *

List, list, the oft-repeated strain
    Of barren craving, senseless hunger!
    Keep, only keep the grievance-monger,
The grievance follows in his train.
A patriot fire within him burns,
    His hand the helm of State must guide,
Or, though the golden age returns,
    He never will be satisfied.

AN INCIDENT IN THE AGRARIAN CAMPAIGN.

THE peasant and the demagogue *
    Were walking hand in hand ;
They wept like anything to see
    The property in land.
" If this were only cleared away,"
    They said, " it would be grand."

" If seven courts on seven scales
    Reduced the rents *each year*,
Do you suppose," the peasant said,
    " We'd pay them ? Never fear ! "

---

* An amateur agitator, who was quite surprised at being " taken " seriously by the police. He had only acted from the most philanthropic motives in " assisting the distressed tenants."

— " The Plan," observed the demagogue,
  " Is most successful here."

The peasant and the demagogue
  Walked on a mile or so,
And rested in a hut from which
  The tenant wouldn't go,
Till all the bailiffs and police
  Came up with bar and crow.

" A loaf of bread," the statesman said,
  " Is what we chiefly need.
Then let the tyrant foe advance,
  We never will recede.
For we are ready, tenants dear,
  Our ' garrison ' to feed."

" The time is come "—the tenant sighed—
  " To talk of many things :
Of brickbats, and of constables,
  And laws of (uncrowned) kings ;

And whether boiling oil is hot,*
　　Or capital has wings."

　　　　*　　*　　*　　*　　*

(*The tenement is taken by storm, and the
　　　demagogue arrested.*)

　　"You don't want me!" the hero whined,
　　Turning a little blue.
　　"All Radicals will think my 'case'
　　Too shocking to be true."
　— "We thank you much," the public said;
　　"Three months you'll kindly do."

　　　　　　　　　　St. J. G., 1889.

"If he had spoken to them of getting ready the boiling oil, it was only in a jocose manner."—*Evidence of an Irish Priest before the Parnell Commission.*

THE PASSIONATE FEMALE-SUFFRAGIST TO HIS LOVE.

COME vote with me, and be my peer,
    Electress and electioneer,
And taste the joys the hustings yield
To all who England's franchise wield.

Then shalt thou sit on local boards,
And rule creation's upstart lords ;
Chair-woman of some Council be,
And p'r'aps—who knows?—at last, M.P.

Each privilege thou'lt practise then
That marks the British citizen ;
If hooting roughs thou dost not fear,
Come vote with me, and be my peer.

Her Answer.

If all the powers of men should rust,
And leave them worthless of our trust,
I should be bound—it follows clear,
To vote *against thee* as thy peer.

But sith I know nor care a groat
For half the things on which ye vote;
And all the better half, I see
Men understand as well as we.

And as the heats of party passion
Inflame already half the nation,
And private peace, not public strife,
Is meet for woman and for wife;

Why, still, in spite of theories sound,
I've no enthusiasm profound—
All things considered, Damon dear—
To vote with thee, and be thy peer.

THE LEGISLATIVE "ORGAN."*

SEATED long since at the "organ,"
    I strummed in a weary way,
And my fingers wandered widely
    For a popular air to play.
I know not of what I was dreaming,
    Though I strive to explain it still,
But I struck one chord of faction
    Like the sound of a Home Rule Bill.

It flooded the House and the Empire,
    Like a fantasy wild and new,
And it shattered my peerless party,
    Like a thunderbolt from the blue.

* "The capacity of our legislative organ is limited, and its strength overtaxed. . . . . The Irish problem necessarily occupies the immediate future."—*Rt. Hon. W. E. Gladstone.*

And I strove to "re-model" the discord
    Of passions I could not cool,
Till I gave up my seat at the organ
    Where I might not play Home Rule.

And yet on that worn-out organ
    I shall strike that chord once more,
And sing in life's sunlit gloaming
    The song that I learnt of yore.
And the law of the land shall quaver
    In tune to a plundering plan,
When the grand old English organ
    Throbs again to the Grand Old Man.

St. J. G., Jan., 1889.

A CONUNDRUM.*

WOULD you see a monster?
　　Step into my house.
Here's a "loathly reptile"
　　And a "creeping louse."
Mind the "rav'ning vulture,"
　　"Vampire" dread beware,
And the "Bengal tiger"
　　In the easy-chair.
At your side's "the foulest
　　Of all beasts of prey."
Tell me if you'd rather
　　Call another day.

* The epithets and synonyms made use of in this poem are carefully selected from the much larger stock which form the glossary of the agrarian agitator.—*Vide* Reports of Evidence before the Parnell Commission, and Nationalist Journals, *passim.*

35

Read my little fable
  (He who runs may read),
I'm the beast, the vampire,
  All the monstrous breed.
Ha! you start and shudder?
  Now, you understand?

—Yes, I own an acre
  Of Hibernian land.

LINES ATTRIBUTED TO

WILLIAM EWART ALEXANDER *SELL-KIRK.* *

ONCE monarch—each word that I said
    Was hailed an infallible bull ; †
But alas ! I am basely betrayed
    By the party that bowed to my rule.
Popularity, where are the charms
    Politicians have seen in thy face ?
Come, " civilized world," to my arms ; ‡
    I abandon this barbarous race.

---

* Mr. Gl-dst-ne's promises of Disestablishment were a mere bribe to the Scotch voters in return for their support on the Home Rule question.—*Speech of Lord Hartington.*

† " The idea of Mr. Gl-dst-ne as a political Pope is a ridiculous invention of the Tory party."—*Daily News.*

‡ " The civilized world is on our side."—*W. E. G.*

I am out of all argument's reach,
　　I must finish my journey alone;
Never read a "dissentient" speech,
　　But silently pore o'er my own.
How Hartington, Chamberlain rant
　　And swear we shall never agree!
They are so unaffected by cant,
　　Their frankness is shocking to me.

How swift are the changes of mind!
　　Compared to my principles' flight
Little Randolph himself lags behind,
　　And what can I think of John Bright?
My friends—if I still have a friend,
　　So far from what once was my home—
Yes, the *Daily News*, true to the end,
　　Still follows wherever I roam.

Constitutions, Religion, and Law,
    Divinely bestowed upon man :
— I can find in the Charter a flaw,
    And defend an agrarian "plan."
So I smile in a reverend way
    While reading the lessons in church,
Could the Baptists my favours repay,
    Poor St-ph-n* I'd leave in the lurch.

But Herbert has gone to his nest,
    The reporter is snoring, I vow :
I must soon be retiring to rest,
    As I've said once or twice before now.
There are factions in every place,
    Hibernian, Cymric, and Scot ;
And the wrongs of religion and race
    Must reconcile me to my lot.

                (1886.)

---

* Presumably the Rev. St-ph-n Gl-dst-ne, Rector of H-w-rd-n.

CONTENTMENT.

An Ode by an Un-*enfranchised Lease-holder.*

MINE be a cot in some fair vill
    (Built by a duke when rents were high),
Or house, or mansion, what you will,
    That I should *like*, but cannot buy.

There would I sign a contract plain,
    That seemed a tenancy for years,
Though to the deep "progressist" brain
    It is not quite what it appears.

Then, while paid agitators sum
    The wrongs of all by leases bound,
Mine ear shall catch the soothing hum
    Of councils legislating round.

No rent-collector's foul attacks
    Shall break my rest on quarter-day;
But swelling " unearned "-Income Tax
    Fright the land-tyrant from his prey.

There, all unsummoned, let me live,
    All unevicted let me die,
Steal from the world, and calmly give
    Sense, Fact, and Law the lie.

A NURSERY RHYME.

(Attributed to the Earl of Caernarvon.)*

Bar, bar *black sheep*,
    Sending out the writs,
Be our legislators
    Statesmen, scholars, wits.

One for the Tory peer,
    And one for the " Rad.,"
But none for the noble lord
    That's gone to the bad.

---

* On the occasion of a proposed reform in the House of Lords, 1889.

A WAIL FROM "NEW TIPPERARY."*

AY me! for the "New Tipperary,"
   And its glories that are not but seem,
Great edifice, golden and airy,
   That vanishes now like a dream.
Where trade should have grown grows the thistle,
   These huts, like our hopes, are decayed;
'Tis quite doleful to hear the wind whistle
   Down the "William O'Brien Arcade."

---

* A collection of wooden buildings erected at the instigation of political agitators, by the misguided tenants of Mr. Smith Barry, notoriously, and by their own admission, one of the best and most considerate of landlords. For a glowing description of the foundations and construction of the New Jerusalem of thievery and tyranny described by this bombastic title, the reader is respectfully invited to refer to the back files of the *Daily News*, from which the dishonesty of the whole proceeding will be abundantly apparent. In May, 1891, this ruinously expensive enterprise had, from its own inherent and gratuitous folly, already collapsed, having cost the Irish people £50,000. "Money was sunk in the William O'Brien Arcade" wrote Mr. James Carew, a former tenant of the estate, in a pathetic letter to the *Times*, "which is now untenanted."

Was our rod of oppression like iron
    When peacefully paying our rent,
Ere ye came, Honest John, and O'Brien,
    And stirred this divine discontent?
And we heeded your bribes and your ravings
    Half believing, and oh! half afraid,
And invested our hardly-earned savings
    In your "William O'Brien Arcade."

Ah! fools of "agrarian feeling"*
    Not to see that, in spite of your cant,
The end of all lying and stealing
    Is remorse, destitution, and want;
That while flourishing Anarchy's flambeau
    Your promises, easily made,
Were as empty, *O arcades ambo*,
    As is "William O'Brien's Arcade."

* "An 'agrarian feeling' seems to mean a desire to get possession of some one else's property for nothing. I will undertake to find you an agrarian feeling anywhere in the streets of London."—*The Marquis of Salisbury.*

BURCHIELLO TO JANE TOMPKINS.

A DRAMATIC IDYLL.*

By the author of "My Fright of a Duchess," "Adventures and Exhaustion" (a transcript of Apollonius Rhodius), "Read Got-on-nightcap Country," "De Gustibus; or, Drams and Scruples," "Glove among the Bruins," "Waring away," "Two Loves and a Wife," "Fortù—*weren't there*," Soliloquy by a Spanish Oyster, "Shop," "Impenetrability," "Rabbi's Tales and Jews d'Esprit," "Tribonian on Asbestos," "Riddle to an Old Lady of Tripoli," "Three in a Coracle," "Two in a Bath-chair," "Gardening Fancies on Bi-furcation," "My Stars!" and many others.

B̲UZZWUZZ! ... Shall he swing on—a murderous
    spider
Scotching the muse on my leaf-hedged window-sill?

---

* Both the metre and the rhymes of this poem have been patented. In regard to a less important point—the meaning—any reader who positively cannot discern it for himself, is respectfully referred to a brochure entitled "*Playtime with a Pen*" (MacMillan & Bowes, Cambridge), recently published by the author, in which the above lines appear, with a commentary, under the title of a "*Dramatic Idyll Reviewed*," and also to some observations of the late Dean

What if Love grew shorter (as he grows wider)
  Curdling a temper once sweet, now indocile.
(No, not yours, *Bildad.*) Heart heart defied? (Ugh !)
  Had she denied her
Moth-kisses—pho ! when yon whiskered corsair
Could drag her downstairs by a three-plait horsehair ?

" Varmint !" I call him, " Virginian (ha !) *creeper!* "
  (And if Pussycats sniffed at their own valerian
Down on my hearthrug, how long would she purr ?)
  —But you think silence the true criterion ?
Well, rather than shut up the lovely *Beau*-peeper
  (Long may her sheep err !)
You can fancy my watching that mincing minx stand
Just within range of my brass-bound inkstand !

Church (see his essays), *apropos*, if we recollect right, of *Sordello.* Before condemning *any* poem as hopelessly unintelligible the reader must be careful to give it a fair chance. Let him read the above lines aloud with an intelligent and sympathetic inflexion, and a proper attention to punctuation and *grammar*, and watch the *effect*. If each hearer will make a short note of his or her idea of the significance of the poem, and compare this with the " Key " aforesaid (price eighteen pence), the author will be directly benefited.

For last year, when we rode by, you vowed—" It *is* hard"
—Thro' the ripe June lilies we heard the brat tick—
That I could not pluck you that grey-winged lizard
   That croaks in the grass of the damp Carnatic.
So you fancied a tale spun, as I'm no wizard,
      Out of one's gizzard.
As if tantrums (Go' bless us!) that tweaked one soul awry
Could smooth out the past like this long-cramped scrollery.

So I peered from my palace (*hic ipse boss sum*)
   Till in earth-attire she came prancing there,
While the gold sun-torrents flashed flix- and floss-some
   Down nebulous fugues of her dappled hair.
Hers? Was it *his?* But a fringe—*non possum*—
     Cut straight across? *Hum.*
"Christiani est."—*What's that?* G-r-r-r! Ignosco.
Huic but not *hic*, though perhaps at Moscow.

How Nature snores in our hot moat-garden !
To the thorough-bass chorus the brown bee-folk hums
I could thrum in a ninth like some cloaked guitar-Don,
Singing—*St!* by the limes her green parasol comes—
But for souls in hammocks that hang and harden,
Fixed in some far den,
(He's one of those) would it all seem quicker work
Than Schireddin's doll toys, feathers and wickerwork?

Hola ! *Pipa di Bacco!* A caïque gliding
Under our prow—(the eleven must know it)
From San Pozzi's duomo you caught the sly *Ding-
Dong o' the nine?* A last tryst ! Be no whit
Blunter, good stile, (Ben Cellini's tried in
Necknape dividing)
Than the—*Skwumpsh!* (He liked eels.)—For her false
swan-throttle,
Well—rage, unlike love, grows stronger in bottle

—Bursting at last.　On those muffled kisses!

　(Cold? Yes, for August—you've tried merino?)

Through the land-lark's carol one voice I miss is

　Caught in rose-meshes no more to flee?　No,

Home up the hill-side (in love's last pthises

　　Cropped up Ulysses!)

Flower o' the turnip!　So deep I've sunk "ohs"

I could dance out the moon in my grandsire's trunkhose.

Foul fiends ha' your *firedogs!* (catch that paraffin,

　'Ere Vulcan and Vishnu o'er Turkey triumph)

No matter—I'd pitchfork the globe's West half in

　For a kink of those curls once ere you *dye* (umph!)

Then alone I roaming Bantry to Baffin

　　(You nectar quaffing)

Can't hope by my losses to re-arrange his?

No, not on this side of our blue chalk-ranges.)

Married—you gander ! What cards for calling ?
  Adela Tompkins (*née* Jane) *Plantagenet* (?!)
A cricket in tears to a cockroach squalling
  Were passion and pain with more true presage in it.
The sea hath prawns, and the dull red shore ling,
    (Darkness is falling)
But love to a life that has loved its fill owes
A *something* perchance to be borne o'er the billows.

St. J. G., 1889.

MY LOVE'S HAT.

The Song of a Season.

MY love she hath a summer hat :
    'Tis like a little boat,
A fairy shallop, broad and flat,
    That on her head doth float.
Upon the billows of her hair
    It resteth ; 'tis so wide,
That I must tell you of the fare
    It carrieth inside.

For first sits in the corner,
    'Mid many a grassy tuft,
A swallow,* like Jack Horner
    (He's dead, of course, and stuffed).

---

* "A bird in the hat is worth two in the bush."—*Mem. for milliners.*

Three fuchsias and an ivy-bush
    (A cargo, you'll allow),
And something else, I think a thrush,
    That carols in the bow.

A beetle, and a butterfly,
    In gold and silver trim,
Swarm up the blue convolvuli
    That dangle on the brim.
There's velvet, lace—but I should sing
    A week—nay, more than that,
'Ere I could tell you everything
    My love hath in her hat.

My love she carries on her head
    This little fairy boat;
But you must judge, from what I've said,
    If it would really float.

'Tis on her head; I've mentioned that,
  But yet I must declare,
You would not know it was a hat
  Unless you saw it there.

LINES

Suggested by the sight of a young Law Student in Fleet Street.

HAIL ! smiling youth, with downy cheek
    And cloudless brow serene,
Why hither tend thy steps? Dost seek
    A second College-green?
Or com'st thou townwards to acquire
    (At Custom's stern command)
A grace, a name, and then retire
    To ornament the land?

The Benchers bid thee to their board—
    Go, take thy lower seat ;
Nor grudge to swell their hostel's hoard,
    But meekly pay and eat.

The world will know (and this redounds
    Much to your young renown)
That once you had a hundred pounds,
    And sometimes dined in town.

Ambitious art thou? Thee we urge
    Go study day and night,
From toil's grim furnace to emerge
    A trenchant blade of might;
That, discontent with wordy play,
    And sick of mimic strife,
Shall carve through all this crowded fray
    A way to larger life.

Say—holds thy soul the quenchless fire
    To cheer thee in that fight,
Immortal Faith, supreme Desire
    That smiles in Fate's despite?

Canst bear thy own—a rival's—fame,
  Nor burn with pride or gall,
Play every hazard of the game,
  And triumph over all?

Bold Templar of the downy chin,
  We love thy blooming cheek;
May many a knight from this old Inn
  Ride forth such prize to seek,
Nor conquering fail the purpose high
  That striving he foresaw;
—Nor swell the whit'ning bones that lie
  About the ways of Law.

A BALLAD OF THE THAMES.

HERE under the ash-tree—beneath the wall,
    My boat lies moored, and I dream at will;
And shadows wrought with reflections fall
    In a quivering maze on the waters still.

And I muse and dream, as the shadows fall
    In a shimmering maze on the waters green,
And I wonder where on the earth's wide ball
    I could sit and gaze on a lovelier scene

Than the broadening stream, where no rush stirs,
    And the white kine dotting the level leas;
And the far hedge broken by dusky firs,
    And the faint blue tufts of the willow-trees.

    *   *   *   *   *

Ho, Mississippi, and Rhine, and Po,
    And Don, and Dnieper, and Guadalquivir,
And all brave waters that seawards flow,
    Can one of you rival our royal river?

Oh never—when lusty Autumn's horn
    The laughing valley's rich lap doth fill,
And purple clover and golden corn
    Stream down the hollow and crown the hill.

And Sport joins Labour—a merry rout,
    And the peasant halts by his laden wain,
At the whistle shrill, and the far faint shout,
    And the dull shots breaking across the plain,

—In Winter I'll grant you that fierce and black
    The South winds storming in squadrons go,
And strewing our fields with ruinous wrack,
    Burst open the stores of the hoarded snow.

Till a mighty lagoon spread waste and wide
    To the feet of the brown hills far withdrawn,
And in tawny furrows the swinging tide
    Lashed round the elm on the flooded lawn;

Then seawards and earthwards delved and died,
    And left a wilderness dank and drear;
Where Nature deep in her breast might hide
    The unbought wealth of the coming year.

But in Spring—oh, who should paint the gleam
    —('Neath the rampart of woodlands fleck'd and pale)
Of the steel-blue scimitar of the stream
    That cuts the pure sward of the virgin vale.

When fruit-blossoms smile through the sunny showers,
    Or strew the wet grass with a crimson pall,
And a thousand towers of its milk-white flowers
    Built up the bright mosque of the chestnut tall.

And in Summer,--at dawn—when cool mists grey
  That veiled the broad Thames with a fairy grace,
By the full fierce sunbeams are purged away
  From the burnished brass of his breathless face.

And in one still mirror the Abbey sleeps,
  And the branching limes, and the poplars tall,
And the dark high roof where the ivy creeps,
  And the sunburnt streaks on the glowing wall.

And towering elms hide all the park,
  But below (where the fretting horses feed)
Their thick stems serry like columns dark
  The sunlit squares of the golden mead.

Breast-deep the cattle stand still and stare
  At the cooling wave, in the burning time,
And the sheep lie crouched in their dusty lair
  'Neath the broad arcade of the humming lime;

And shadows mixt with reflections fall
  (Where my boat lies moored) on the waters green,
And I wonder where on the earth's round ball
  You could sit and gaze on a lovelier scene

Than the broadening stream, where no rush stirs,
  And the white kine dotting the level leas;
And the far hedge broken by dusky firs,
  And the faint blue tufts of the willow-trees.

So—Mississippi, and Rhine, and Rhone,
  And Po, and Dnieper, and Guadalquivir,
I take your silence to freely own
  That none of you rival our royal river.

Bisham, May 15, 1892.

THE LAUREATE AT BAY.*

YOU are treating me severely, most severely, Collins dear,
Your book will be the greatest "boom" of all the dying year;
Of all the crowded year, Collins, the maddest, merriest say,
For I'm to be shorn of the bay, Collins, I'm to be shorn of the bay.

---

* In his "Illustrations of Tennyson," Mr. John Churton Collins has collected a number of the original sources from which Lord Tennyson has enriched his poetry. . . . . Mr. Collins proves rather too much. . . . . It is to be feared that, in spite of his protests, the general public will be impressed with the belief that the Laureate is a plagiarist.—*Daily Paper*.

There'll be many a black, black name, Collins, but none
    so black as mine,
There's Mr. L——s M——s, and all the scribbling line;
But of all the imitative bards, I'm worst by a long, long
    way,
I take it that's what you say, Collins, that's what you
    mean to say.

I never thought a single soul could be so wide awake;
You might have "called me earlier" to such a grave
    mistake;
I must really look up something original some day,
Or I shall be shorn of my bay, Collins, shorn of the
    Laureate's bay.

There's Homer and Theocritus, and many, many more,
I never thought to pilfer, adapting from their store—
Adapting, mark you, Collins, in a Tennysonian way;
But there—I'm shorn of the bay, Collins, I'm to be shorn
    of the bay.

Of course you won't believe it, you'll do just as you
    please,
But I never stole a single word from Aristophanes.
And don't you think, my Collins—it seems to me so
    clear—
That two great minds might hit for once upon the same
    idea?

Within my Sophocles, Collins, you'll find the marker left,
But of my "fiery crocus," oh, 'tis hard to be bereft!
And I may have read the line, Collins (it isn't *quite* the
    same),
Or thought of Wordsworth's "flowrets that set the hills
    aflame."

Ill-fated "Oriana"—I dreamed she was my own,
Tho' "Helen of Kirkconnell Lea" was not to me unknown.
But as to flowers and grasses, and cloudlets in the sun,
I know their looks as well as you, or Peele, or any one.

My time, I think, is over. Perhaps, and yet I know
The simple hearts of England I've thrilled with many a
    glow.
You'll comfort them, my Collins, as I could not do *alone*
(Suppose you write them something that's every bit your
    own).

I have been wild and wayward in the "sources" whence
    I've "drawn"
(I never prigged from Spencer, nor yet from Henry
    Vaughan);
But if I write again, Collins, I'll think of what you say,
Or I shall be shorn of the bay, Collins, I shall be shorn
    of the bay.

Globe, Nov. 30, 1891.

AFTER BRET HARTE.

"I WRITE for *Punch*," the young man said:
    Quoth the Editor, "Nay, no more,
You are doubtless the high-class humourist
    That for years we've been looking for."

"I write for *Punch*," the young man sighed:
    —"But which is your line of all?
The paragraph pun, or the comical notes,
    Or the songs for the music hall?"

"I write for *Punch*," that young man said:
    Quoth the Editor, "Yes, quite so,
But it hardly can occupy all your time,
    And we don't want much, you know:

"If you've got the talent, the happy knack
    That have made that Journal's fame,
For a 'skit' or a parody now and then,
    We will thank you all the same."

"I write for *Punch*—and for ten long years
    I have sent them joke and pun
(Here his tone grew sad), but I ought to add,
    That they've never inserted one."

The Editor spake him never a word,
    But plied his whistle-call;
"Show out that young man who writes jokes for
    Punch
    That never appear at all."

THE "LEADING MAGAZINE."

Lines of Advice to a Literary Aspirant, by G. A. (author of "The Girl of the *Few-cheer*," "Poverty and Periwinkles," "The Mythical Celt," and numerous other contributions to the *Extempore Review* and the late *Youneversell Magazine*.)

Do you want to print an article
   No mortal can defend,
Where not of sense one particle
   Is found from end to end,
Which once the world has read it o'er
   You'll wish had never been?
Then hasten to the Editor
   Of a "Leading Magazine."

I'll assume your appellation's
   Known to journalistic fame
(Singular excogitations
   Suit a striking double name).

Though you bore us to satiety
  By asserting what is not ;
Yet of needful notoriety,
  Rubbish serves to boil the pot.

Go, then, frantically twaddle,
  Or illogically gush,
Or evolve from out your noddle
  What will make the printer blush.
Though your wife will long to hide it
  Where it never can be seen,—
Never mind—you have supplied it
  To a "Leading Magazine."

Would you like to show how marriage
  Is the source of all our ills,
Every faith and creed disparage,
  Prove one needn't pay one's bills?

Do but shock dull minds respectable
By some bolt from sky serene,
And you'll just be thought delectable
In a "Leading Magazine."

Take the worst and most surprising
Of the things you don't believe ;
Then your cynic sneers disguising,
Some fantastic theory weave ;
hough of fact it boasts no basis,
And you don't know what you mean,
You'll be welcomed with embraces
In a " Leading Magazine."*

Globe, 1891.

---

* "Such a contribution," observed the *Standard*, of an astonishingly ignorant and silly effusion hight "The Nationalization of Cathedrals" (not by G. A., this time) "could hardly have obtained admission to a Leading Magazine except in the dead season." We hope so. The cases here referred to are doubtless discreditable exceptions to editorial rules.

THE LAY OF THE ADVERTISER.

Air: "I shall be there."

I SHALL be there :—'mid the hubbub and cry
    Of the thronged thoroughfare
Blatant I blare. At my hoarding on high
    Artists may glare.
Little reck I, with my Soap, and my Pill, and my Wash
    for the Hair,
    I shall be there ! I shall be there !

I shall be there—in each sandwich-clad guy,
    Shape foul or fair,
Vehicle rare—(causing horses to shy,
    Rustics to stare,
Babies to cry)—in my car upon wheels or balloon in the
    air,
    Touting some ware, I shall be there !

Forth when ye fare, by the road or the rail,
    Lo! I am there,
On each wall bare Mustard and Ale
    Racing in pair.
Passengers pale for each station's name shriek, whimpering, "Where?"
    What do I care, so *I* am there?

I shall be there, in the hearth and the home,
    Everywhere!
Spring from my lair at the close of each tome—
    Cut me who dare!
Vainly ye roam; in each journal or print, if an inch be to spare
    (So much the square), I shall be there!

"BALLADE."*

SEEK not through all my gilded ream
 Or sober sense, or thought sincere ;
Of fancy not one living gleam
 Doth light my verse from far or near.
 Wit, passion, purpose never fear,
In my serenely soulless lay :
 Yet must I sing, and you must hear
The Ballade-monger of the Day.

Some faded flower of Classicism,
 Some literary trifle viewed
Through "shoppy" microscopic prism,
 Some antique plaything, bad or good.

---

*Composed after reading a dainty volume of verse, *on large, hand-made paper, only fifty copies printed* (and quite enough too), royal octavo, half vellum, gilt and gewgawed *ad libitum*, &c., &c., &c.

Great Heaven ! we mean not to be rude,
But—Booklet, Ballade, Triolet !—
   Not bards, bookmakers shallow-shrewd,
Thus pour the artificial lay.

Scarce did they prattle in such form,
   Scarce of such nothings did they sing ;
The silly Courtier-poet swarm
   About the Great (but little) King.
   Our life is grown a sterner thing :
We rhyme and smile, and are not gay.
   In truth, it has a shallow ring,
The modern Ballade-monger's Lay.

And do these echoes false and vain
   Express our jaded world's desire ?
Perhaps. Yet is not this the strain
   That throbbed to Villon's tears of fire.

The thought provokes a quenchless ire,
Go, rhymers, rhyme another way;
  In silence tune a fuller lyre,
And strike a lusty English Lay.

O *blasé* reader, thoughtless buyer,
  Shake off this Lang-uor of a day;
With ballade-booklets light your fire,
  And call a hearty English Lay.

Camb. Rev.

THE MODERN ARMOURER'S CAROL.

By the Author of " Ye Carpette Knighte."

I HAVE a gonne, a ryghte bigge gonne,
    I wis 'twould you surprise ;
It shooteth balles of half a tonne
    Amonge ye enemies !
(But yette, I sweare, you're safer there
    When into byttes it flies.)

I have a sworde, a German sworde ;
    Nay, feare not for your life,
It splinters like ye dealy boarde
    In tyme of bloudie stryfe ;
But it will make without mistake
    A rattlynge paper-knife.

A bayonette, too, I have ryghte newe
    (A riche contractor's worke),
To thrust and poke it will not doe
    More than ye hemlocke stalk ;
But it will bend (my lay to ende)
    Into a toasting-forke !

                    St. J. G., 1889.

IN THE ZOO.

By a " Minor" Poet.

I TELL you in a rhyming way
    Of how we went the other day
To call on creatures at the Zoo,
As country children cannot do.

The frisky little antelope
Has curlywurly horns that slope ;
It lives on buns, they quite agree,
And Mabel gave it one for me.

Nurse lets her ride (she says I can't)
Upon the toppling effelaunt,
With skin so very thick and stout,
It quackles when he walks about.

The lioness stands up to roar,
You hear it far outside the door,
She seems to strain her very chest *
To show how deeply she's distressed.

The jaguar—oh, do you see?
Is fast asleep up on his tree; †
His eyes are closed with solemn frown,
They'll open if he tumbles down.

The yellow tiger licks his jaws,
And winks at me across his paws;
The little pumas jump and play,
Their hearts are very light and gay.

---

* The contralto notes of the lion are never formed in the head or throat, but are all "chest notes," thus involving a great and unnecessary strain on the system.

† March 22, 1890. The animal will certainly break its neck some day.

The lion eats with hearty will,
But *cannot* keep his mutton still; *
He really doesn't seem to know
That baby wouldn't hold it so.

The seal has caught such lots of fish,
He does exactly what you wish ;
To tumble never frightens him,
He is so sure that he can swim.

The monkeys and the screeching bird,
And other reptiles most absurd,
We talk about them in the 'bus—
(I hope they'll keep some tea for us).
Camb. Rev.

---

* The creature's attempts to do so are quite ridiculous; the keepers should give it a fork.

TO AN EMINENT LITTÉRATEUR:

On reading his own account of his early education contributed to " Scribner's Magazine."

AND were the famed " Arabian Nights
    Your childhood's earliest heaven?
And could you try Shakespearean flights
    When you were barely seven?
And did you find when older grown
    You loved " Sir Walter " so,
Though " better boys " (as yet unknown
    To us) pronounced him " slow "?

The Minstrel's Lay you mastered soon?
    Nor found your fancy cloyed
By " Stag at eve " and " dancing moon "
    You read, and quite enjoyed

The Tournament (I'm glad you told
    Us that), nor turned away
From "Ivanhoe" and Quentin bold,
    And Front-de-Bœuf at bay?

And next you tasted Thackeray,
    And loved the "Rose and Ring"?
[You will excuse me if I say
    That *was* a funny thing!]
The "Christmas Carol," what! as well,
    You found a perfect treat?
And Hiawatha wove a spell?
    And Tennyson was sweet?

But I must add, if this was so
    (Such vanity you'll blame),
Like other persons that I know,
    I used to do the same.

Yet if the tale I should indite,
   The world would cry " Go hang!"
But then I'm not a famous wight,
   And you are—A ***** L ***.

P. M. G., Sept. 12, 1891.

A SONG OF SELF-DEFENCE.

By a Conscientious Householder.*

BURGLAR, burgling in my hall—
Ere I launch this fatal ball,
Is my worst suspicion true?
Or, if not, then *who are you?*

By this dim and flickering lamp
Say you're not a tipsy tramp.

Even during the hours of night, as legally defined in the case of burglary (9 p.m. to 6 a.m.), the householder will do well not to take the initiative until he is sure that his nightly visitant has felonious intentions and is not a mere accidental trespasser. His legal position will be still more unimpeachable if, instead of perhaps taking some harmless individual by surprise, he waits or "retires" until he is attacked or driven to bay in some place where further retreat is impossible, or put positively "in terror of his life," before shooting at the supposed burglar.—*Vide Correspondence in* "*Standard*" *during burglary season* 1889-90.

If we join the wild assault,
Mine—or *yours* the legal fault?

Burglar with the ugly mask,
Tell me true—'tis all I ask
(I'm not sure my watch is right),
Is it "day," or is it "night"?

With this Blackstone in my hand,
Here, "at bay," I'll take my stand.
With the law I'd fain comply,
Put your Colt's revolver by.

Burglar, burglar on the stairs,
I won't take you unawares.
Now three times I've spoken plain,
Answer ere you fire again.

Burglar, that was rather near:
—Say, my heart, can this be fear?
Yes, my nerves with horror thrill!
Now I'll shoot at Burglar Bill.

HORATIAN ODE.

DEAR Fuscus, though the thought may jar,
    Deep-lying truths we must not blink them :
Our ills we feel not as they are,
    But as we think them.

Dull trade the merchant doth deplore,
    But, while for countless gold he itches,
Not Poverty doth make him poor,
    But Rothschild's riches.

With cold I sniff : ah ! gruesome lot !
    Yet Fortune kind in mercy sends a
Consoling sorrow—Jones has got
    The Influenza !

We're ne'er alone—in griefs or chills
   (To human sufferers that is *the* pill)—
So let us "grin and bear" the ills
   —Of other people.

'Tis not unkindness :—friends, perverse
   Your healthful joys who'd spurn unheeded,
Quite pleased, will stay up nights to nurse
   You invalided.

Lo! warmer climes the wealthy seek
   (By voyaging man can't escape ills);
I read with scarce a pang, last week,
   Of snow in Naples.

Oh! there's a subtle joy that steals,
   And some un-altruistic chord tunes
In every heart that rightly feels
   A friend's misfortunes.

Blest fellow-beings ! o'er whose pain
    The sympathetic tear we yet shed :
We suffer less since you, 'tis plain,
    May be more wretched.

Then think of others : human kind
    Nor great nor small misfortunes may shun ;
The remedy is—undesigned
    Co-operation.

AT A POST-OFFICE.

*Inadvertently omitted from "Ballads and Lyrics"
by Mr. G—rge M—r—d—th.*

I HEARD that morn from Mr. Cox,
    Then, like a bursting dam,
I cantered round the square to box
    My sprawling cryptogram.

Unmarked I " hammered striding legs "
    Against the swinging door,
It hurt. (This phrase attention begs,)
    My snorting temper swore.

Miss knitted on, beatified
    In Post-official calm;
The Psalmist could not more have tried
    To break her head with balm.

I listened to her Sunday-frock
    And tales of other men—
Now Hurry is a fighting-cock,
    But " Patience is a hen."

A vandal vile had worse abhorred
    Her merry mood to damp;
I shrieked across the shuddering board,
    " *I want a penny stamp!*"

Appeased by pinky lips that pout,
    I let my " laughter neigh "—
(For which expression I took out
    A Patent t'other day).

It struck me sharply once or twice
  (This figure's rich and rude),
That gnarlèd Slang I'd like to splice
  With tinkling Platitude.

Prose-poems plough the puny pate;
  But, give a fellow time,
I'm hoping shortly to translate
  My novels into rhyme.

TO A THOUGHTFUL EDITOR.*

OF all your literary store,
    The "leader," friend, I most abhor;
In pointed "pars." oh, kindly chip it,
And let me revel in my "snippet."

Though sagely grave and brightly gay
The gist and style of what you say,
In sugared spoonfuls let me sip it,
The jaded sense prefers the "snippet."

---

* "Though the general public are not aware of it, they take to the 'snippet' because it keeps them from thinking, and stick to it because it has made them unable to think. They will by-and-bye insist upon all parliamentary reports, all leading articles being put into paragraphs, and the thoughtful proprietor will yield to their demands."—*Scots Observer.*

Then bid me not o'er columns pore
Of news or diplomatic lore ;
Each startling fact you'll kindly flip it
Straight down my throat in form of "snippet."

To read, to weigh, to judge, decide,
Too often have we vainly tried ;
Fond effort ! in the bud oh, nip it
With one condensed exhaustive " snippet."

Kind friend, how few can spare the time
With facts or thoughts their minds to prime !
In truth's deep well your pen pray dip it,
Give us all wisdom in a " snippet."

ODE TO THE ELECTRIC LIGHT AT THE GREAT WESTERN RAILWAY TERMINUS.

TWINKLE, twinkle little Arc,
    Sickly, blue, uncertain spark;
Up above my head you swing,
Ugly, strange, expensive thing!

Now the flaring gas is gone
From the realms of Paddington,
You must show your quivering light,
Twinkle, blinkle left and right.

When across the foggy air
Streams the lightning's purple glare;
Does the traveller in the dark
Bless your radiance, little Arc?

When you fade with modest blush,
Scarce more bright than farthing rush,
Would he know which way to go
If you always twinkled so?

Cold, unlovely, blinding star,
I've no notion what you are,
How your wondrous "system" works,
Who controls its jumps and jerks.

Yours a lustre like the day!
Ghastly, green, inconstant ray!
No; where'er they worship you,
All the world is black or blue.

Though your light perchance surpass
Homely oil or vulgar gas,
Still (I close with this remark)
I detest you, little Arc!

CONVERSATIONAL DITTIES.

I.—THE FLAT JOKE.

BLANK silence falls,
   Its weight appals
      The *conteur* in his fleeting glory.
No hearer takes
The point, or wakes
      To greet the crisis of the story.
Laugh, prithee, laugh; set the kind echoes flying;
Will no one break the silence, trying, trying, trying?

II.—THE MAN WHO KNOWS.

He grasps the facts, with waving hand,
And, sphynx-like, putteth questions bland,
That no one else can understand.

The twaddling crew beneath him sprawls,
The fallacy he swift forestalls,
Then, like a thunderbolt, he falls.

THE END.

www.ingramcontent.com/pod-product-compliance
Lightning Source LLC
Chambersburg PA
CBHW030052170426
43197CB00010B/1494